BIGGER KINGDOM
OR BIGGER BARNS

BIGGER KINGDOM
OR BIGGER BARNS

Estate Planning from
a Biblical Perspective

Dan Celia
Forward by Dr. Woodrow Kroll

TATE PUBLISHING & *Enterprises*

Published by Tate Publishing & Enterprises, LLC
127 E. Trade Center Terrace | Mustang, Oklahoma 73064 USA
1.888.361.9473 | www.tatepublishing.com

Tate Publishing is committed to excellence in the publishing industry. The company reflects the philosophy established by the founders, based on Psalm 68:11,
"The Lord gave the word and great was the company of those who published it."

Book design copyright © 2009 by Tate Publishing, LLC. All rights reserved.
Cover design by Tyler Evans
Interior design by Lindsay B. Behrens

Published in the United States of America

ISBN: 978-1-60799-500-5
1. Law / Wills   2. Business & Economics / Strategic Planningy
09.06.02

Dedicated to
All of the individuals
desiring to see the
Kingdom of Jesus Christ grow
and
understanding their part in
that through their giving.

With the greatest appreciation
I give thanks to:
Administrative Assistant:
Pat O'Toole
First Editor: Eric L. Rivera

The Parable of the Rich Fool
Luke 12:13-21 (NKJV)

Then one from the crowd said to Him, "Teacher, tell my brother to divide the inheritance with me." But He said to him, "Man, who made Me a judge or an arbitrator over you?" And He said to them, "Take heed and beware of covetousness, for one's life does not consist in the abundance of the things he possesses."

Then He spoke a parable to them, saying: "The ground of a certain rich man yielded plentifully. And he thought within himself, saying, 'What shall I do, since I have no room to store my crops?' So he said, 'I will do this: I will pull down my barns and build greater, and there I will store all my crops and my goods. And I will say to my soul, "Soul, you have many goods laid up for many years; take your ease; eat, drink, *and* be merry.'" But God said to him, 'Fool! This night your soul will be required of you; then whose will those things be which you have provided?' "So *is* he who lays up treasure for himself, and is not rich toward God."

Table of Contents

Foreword

Does your view of money match God's view? Said differently, are God and you on the same page when it comes to earning, saving, and giving your wealth?

I know, money is one of those topics we're not supposed to talk about; but why not? God has a lot to say in his Word about money. Of our Lord's thirty–six parables, seventeen of them have to do with property and stewardship. Trouble is, most Christians don't know enough about God's Word to know what he says about money. It's hard to get a biblical view of money without reading the Bible. But if you take the time to find out what God has to say, or if you read someone who has taken the time, you'll discover that the key to using your

money in a way that satisfies you, benefits others, and pleases God is always to give the master charge of your wealth.

But first, let's come to terms. When I say "wealth," what do I mean? Is that a term only for those in a higher tax bracket than you? My *Funk and Wagnall's Dictionary* defines wealth as, "A large aggregate of real and personal property; an abundance of those material or worldly things that men desire to possess." I'd say that definition is just about perfect. It certainly catches the spirit of our times.

But beyond dictionary definitions, what does the Bible have to say about your wealth? Think of several things.

First, all wealth belongs to God. That's right. Everything you have, all the wealth you've amassed, really belongs to God. I know that's a difficult concept to swallow today, but the Bible says that everything is created, sustained, and owned by God. In writing a hymn of praise to God, the psalmist acknowledged, "The earth is full of your possessions" (Psalm 104:24). David blessed the Lord before all the Israelites gathered at the temple and said, "For all that is in heaven and in earth is Yours … Both riches and honor come from You" (1 Chronicles 29:11–12). The prophet Haggai quoted the Lord of hosts as saying, "The silver is mine, and the gold is mine" (Haggai 2:8).

Remember that little chorus you used to sing many years ago? It went something like this: "He owns the cattle on a thousand hills, the wealth in every mine." Well, it was true. The question is, do you still believe it?

Second, since all wealth belongs to God, any wealth you have is a gift from him. Again, let's see what the Bible says. Moses was giving his swan song challenge to the people of Israel and said, "And you shall remember the LORD your God, for it is he who gives you power to get wealth" (Deuteronomy 8:18). That's pretty unambiguous. The wisdom found in the Book of Ecclesiastes mirrors these thoughts. "As for every man to whom God has given riches and wealth, and given him power to eat of it, to receive his heritage and rejoice in his labor—this is the gift of God" (Ecclesiastes 5:19).

Ecclesiastes 6:2 makes reference to, "A man to whom God has given riches and wealth and honor, so that he lacks nothing for himself of all he desires." Remember Funk and Wagnall's definition of wealth? Everything you have in "real and personal property" is God's gift to you. All wealth comes from him. You may have worked hard to earn it or invested wisely to earn it, but the bottom line is, you have it because God gifted to you what ultimately belongs to him. So the way you use wealth reflects on how you view God in your life.

In the pages that follow, Dan Celia gives you solid, biblical advice about how to handle this precious gift of wealth God has given you. How you invest, how you save, how you stretch, how you help others, how you give back to God—all these are issues of biblical stewardship and estate planning. God has spoken of them in his Word. Dan incorporates the words of Scripture in "nuts and bolts" advice about how to plan for your future. Estate planning is not just important; it's vital to the integrity of your Christian life.

—Dr. Woodrow Kroll
Back to the Bible
Lincoln, Nebraska

Introduction

For many years on the radio I have talked about the importance of taking a biblical approach to estate planning. For over twenty-five years, I have helped people plan and grow their finances in their financial management and their estate planning and designed trusts and wills that not only would suit their needs but would also create tax advantages and giving advantages. And in that time, I have come to the understanding of how essential it is to provide a detailed road map for how and when our assets should be allocated both before and after the Lord decides to call us home. Even after we have carefully planned for our death, we should be prepared to be constantly updating our wills and estate plans. With a constantly changing tax law (which we know is going to change again in the near future), we have to be thinking long term and thinking ahead.

A biblical perspective to estate planning is centered on God's desire for us to carefully plan. As a matter of fact, Proverbs 15:22 clearly states that *"without counsel and without plans, they* (plans, that is) *will quickly go awry."* (They'll go awry.) *"But in the multitude of counselors, they are established."* Scripture also tells us that it is *"the foolish man who does not plan wisely."* In order to plan wisely and prudently, I believe that we certainly need to be seeking out wise counsel.

Well, what about all the scriptures that tells us not to worry? In Matthew 12:24, Jesus makes it clear that God provides for even the birds of the air. "And of how much more value are you than the birds?" There are many other scriptural references that talk against the idea of building bigger barns or silos in which to store up our wealth. I particularly like Luke's gospel, Chapter 12, where Jesus is speaking the parable of the rich fool. Someone from the crowd comes to Christ and asks him to talk to his brother about dividing up the inheritance with him. Jesus certainly understands that this man is probably asking from a heart of greed, so he says to the man, "Who made me a judge or an arbitrator over you?" Then in Luke 12:15, Jesus turns to the crowd and says to them, "Take heed and beware of covetousness, for one's life does not consist in the abundance of the things he possesses." The first words that he speaks in that verse, "Take heed and beware," tells us a lot about the right perspective we are to have on our things. In verses 17–20 he speaks of a man who has much wealth—a certain rich man who was questioning himself about all his wealth. The man said, "What shall I do, since I have no room to store my crops?" So the man proclaimed, "I will do this: I will pull down my barns and build greater, and there I will store all my crops and my goods. And I will say to my soul, 'Soul, you have many goods laid up for many years; take your ease; eat, drink, and be merry.'" But God said to him, "Fool! This night your soul will be required of you; then whose will those things be which you have provided?" (NKJV).

We, too, have that option. We can continue to do our estate planning with the idea that one of the accomplishments of a well–thought–out estate plan is going to allow us to accumulate and save more of our riches or our goods or those things that God has provided for us. Or we can use those things as an instrument of God to do kingdom work. We have to make a number of decisions, certainly, as we plan our stewardship of our financial resources; and one of those things that we have to decide is— are we going to contemplate how it is we are going to build bigger barns for all of the wealth God has provided to us? Or are we going to be in collaboration with God in growing the kingdom and understand that wealth is determined in one's heart?

To some, wealth could be a lot; to others, little. Are we going to even consider the fact that most of what we are growing will be of little consequence in the kingdom—yes, even growing our money? Let's focus on growing more comfortable in providing for a bigger kingdom, not a bigger barn. I believe the Lord is making it very clear that we can't take our wealth with us, but we can see others come to the kingdom by what we are doing with what the Lord has provided us. That would be laying up eternal wealth. We are not to hoard our resources so that we may have an easy life, let's say, when we retire. But there is a balance. We are to continue to give of our first fruits, first and foremost, to God; and that should never change, regardless of how little we are able to save for our retirement. We are continually to be givers to God and to kingdom work.

When we think of planning for the future, there needs to be a wise, godly, well-thought-out plan; a plan that, prior to beginning it, we would take before the Lord, pray about it, and pray through it as we ask for discernment in developing that plan. I believe that we have the responsibility to plan not only for our estate and heirs but also for the kingdom of Jesus Christ. Paul reminds us in 1 Corinthians 4: "Let a man so consider us as servants of Christ and stewards of the mysteries of God. Moreover it is required of stewards that one be found faithful." Paul is reminding us that we have stewardship responsibility for the mysteries of God. You and I know that "the mysteries of God" is the gospel of Jesus Christ. It is kind of scary to think that we have stewardship responsibility for the gospel. Well, we all can't be preachers, teachers, missionaries, or evangelists, but we can all use the gifts of the fruit that God has provided for us to see that the sacred mysteries of God, the gospel of Jesus Christ, is proclaimed. Christendom needs us to continue to be instruments of God's peace and love to participate in proclaiming the gospel. That means we need to first and foremost be considering a bigger kingdom and a proclamation of the gospel.

Whenever I have an opportunity to speak (in public or on my radio program), I try to make the point that one of my goals is to motivate God's people to give to God's work—to grow the kingdom of Christ. All of our stewardship must be built on the foundation of our responsibility for the Gospel. Not my kingdom and not my ministry, but those ministries that are directly or indirectly proclaiming the gospel and are working toward biblical literacy for all of us. I know that if I can help people make good sound decisions about their finances and investing, they will grow a deeper comfort and a greater ability to give to these ministries.

In the following chapters, we will look at some of the financial challenges in making those plans, some of the ways that the plan truly works for you and your family, and some of the common mistakes and inadequacies that so many estate plans contain.

My desire with this book is to plant a seed in your heart not to forget kingdom work in your planning. As much as we dislike talking about money, we need to understand, not only today but also in future generations, the importance of continuing to finance the important work of biblical literacy and the proclamation of the gospel. Like it or not, it's up to us to see that God's work here at home and around the world continues.

God's Word reminds us: Therefore the disciples said to one another, "Has anyone brought him anything to eat?" Jesus said to them, "My food is to do the will of him who sent Me, and to finish his work. Do you not say, 'There are still four months and then comes the harvest'? Behold, I say to you, lift up your eyes and look at the fields, for they are already white for harvest! And he who reaps receives wages, and gathers fruit for eternal life, that both he who sows and he who reaps may rejoice together. For in this the saying is true: 'One sows and another reaps.' I sent you to reap that for which you have not labored; others have labored, and you have entered into their labors."

John 4:33–38(NKJV)

The harvest that we can reap has eternal value. It is the resources that the Lord has given us that we must use as labors of Christ and stewards of the gospel.

Chapter One

The Will

Simply put, plans fail for lack of planning—Proverbs makes that very clear to us. If we are going to have a good estate plan, it's important that we take certain steps to carefully arrange things the way that *we* would like them to be. The cornerstone of every sound estate plan is a will. Without one, nothing else much matters. Through a will, you can distribute any kind of property that is owned whether it be real estate, antiques, coin collections, or whatever. There are many different ways that you can make distribution of your assets, but once the Lord calls you home, you must rely solely on your will. You should rely on the will that *you* established—not your executor whom you want to settle your estate. Make that person's life as easy as possible and clearly spell out all your possessions and the ways in which you want them distributed and to whom they should go.

Wills and Living Trusts

A will is, of course, a very simple document that lays out your final wishes for the disbursement of your assets, a guardian for your minor children, and how assets are to be set up and managed for those minor children and at what age and or circumstance must be achieved before they become eligible for receipt of those assets. The will also designates who settles the estate executor or executrix. A trust is a bit more complicated. Instead of heirs you will at the time you develop the trust and designate trustees, usually you and your spouse and co–trustees and your death might trigger the closing of the trust, in which time the trustees and any ministries and charities will receive the assets.

Even though you may determine that a living trust is the right estate–planning tool for you, you still need a will. Please don't make the mistakes that many people make when they have a living trust: they feel as though the trust takes care of everything and they do not need a will. You still need to have an executor named in a will to settle your estate. There may be small personal items that you would like people *other than the trustees of the trust* to receive. For instance, you may have a piano that you would like to go to your church. That would not be named in the trust but would, in fact, be named in the will. This type of will, when there is a living trust in place, is called a pour–over will simply meaning that all assets that are not named in the will specifically, or are not named in the trust specifically, would be poured over into the trust and become part of the trust. Keep in mind that this will does not replace the idea of putting the majority of your main assets in the name of the trust. There still must be shown to the IRS an intent that the majority of your assets are intended to be put in the trust.

Another common mistake that so many people make in a living trust is that they do not rename, or re–title, all of their assets in the trust. The pour–over will is simply an instrument that will include things like a car or an antique or other things that are not specifically named in a trust document.

But if any of these things are being distributed to minor children at the time of your death, you also have to provide and make arrangements for a guardian for those minor children. One of the most important aspects of your will is that you don't want the state to appoint the guardian for your children. You could also make a note in a will or a trust when it comes to minor children that the assets that are distributed to those children could be managed by a separate entity. They do not have to be managed by the guardian whom you appoint. You might want the guardian to be responsible for the management of finances. Remember, the will or living trust must be reviewed with an attorney from your state. Please don't do it yourself and just have it notarized. Every state has different laws, and they change often.

Making a Final Tithe

If you are establishing a will, please do not forget the Lord. Don't forget to provide your final tithe. Are we, even in our death, looking to see the kingdom of Christ grow? This subject is very near and dear to me because it is an opportunity, particularly if you have been a faithful giver and a faithful tither throughout your life, to make sure that in your will you provide one last gift to the ministries or church to which you may be providing support now. Take 10 percent of your assets, or more if you would like, and make a note in your will that 10 percent of your assets are to be distributed among the ministries that you have selected and to which you are continuing to give.

I have been living in the same house for twenty-five years. It has greatly appreciated even in the mist of this housing crisis, as the area in which we live has grown dramatically and has become a very desirable place to live. Unfortunately, as faithful as my wife and I try to be in our giving and tithing, I am not in a position to tithe on the appreciation of my home. Therefore, I have made a provision in my will to make my final tithe on all of my assets that would include the appreciation on our home. When it comes to giving to your church, I think it is extremely important that you consider this as well, but I always ask people to write in their wills that they are giving a certain percentage to "the church that I am attending at the time of my death." This is extremely critical because you know, and I know, how much difficulty a church can go through.

There may be a situation, for example, that a few years before the Lord calls you home you may have changed churches. Maybe the church where you were attending has gone in a different direction doctrinally—a direction that you do not believe to be biblical—so you have made a change. But oftentimes you might not have an opportunity to change your will before the Lord calls you home. In this case, if you named a *specific* church, then that church you have left will be receiving your gift, and you may be supporting a church that you would rather not support. So rather than naming a specific church, I always suggest that you write, "The church where I am attending at the time of my death." At this time, you have to depend upon the executor to know what church you are attending and to make distribution to your current church.

One of the things that I always include when I design a draft will for someone's attorney is this opening statement: *For it is by grace you have been saved, through faith—and this is not from yourselves, it is the gift of God—not by works, so that no one can boast. For we are God's workmanship, created in Christ Jesus to do good works, which God prepared in advance for us to do,* Ephesians 2:8–10. Why not make one last testimony? There may be non–believers reading this will or maybe non–believing family members or attorneys or bank representatives. What a great statement of faith to start off the will.

Charitable Giving

Don't forget that you must also consider your charitable giving. What ministries would you like to receive assets, and what percentage of the assets would you like them to receive? I always suggest that you try to narrow down the list of ministries of three or four. Oftentimes we give to ministries that often have the same goals and objectives in mind so that as far as kingdom work goes, you are duplicating your efforts. Try to narrow it down to the ones that you deem most responsible. One of my favorite websites for this is: www.ministry-watch.org. You type in the name of the ministry and it gives you a rating on that ministry; then you can get some great ideas as to whom *not* to give to or whom you should give to. Ultimately it is between you and the Lord, but always give as he leads.

Who Needs a Will?

Please do not get caught up in thinking that a will is only for people who have assets, or that a will is only for people who are wealthy; and don't say, "I am a single individual, so I don't need to have a will." Everyone needs to have a will, regardless of how complex or how simple his or her lifestyle may be. You do not want the state to appoint an executor to settle your estate, regardless of how small you may think it is. You want to be able to determine those distributions yourself.

Also, it is important to understand that in most states the will is going to have to be probated. For instance, in the state of Pennsylvania it is close to 5 percent for a probate tax. One thing that generally triggers the probate is an executor going to the bank and requesting access to a safe deposit box.

In most states, and I know in the state of Pennsylvania, this will most assuredly trigger an audit by a State Representative, and the banking person will then generally take a full inventory of everything that is in the safe deposit box for the sake of probate. In most states there is generally a probate tax due on all of your assets. Some states have a threshold that no tax is due until the amount of assets reaches a certain point. You need to understand what that amount is, and your will needs to be designed accordingly and assets protected to take full advantage of the law.

The question often asked is, "Can I avoid probate tax?" There are certain ways that you can minimize this or there may be certain assets on which you can avoid probate altogether. But this is, again, going to take careful planning with your attorney or your estate–planning representative. One can create living trusts, irrevocable and/or revocable, and have assets placed in those trusts to avoid certain Federal tax and state probate tax, and we will talk about that in a later chapter on trusts.

Naming Your Executor

There are a number of other things that have to be considered when you plan a will. One of these is: Who would be your executor? Who is the person (singular) that you would like to settle your estate? I always suggest that people have an alternate or "successor executor."

I suggest the words in the will to say this: "In the event that *John Smith*, my son, is unable or unwilling to serve as executor, then I hereby appoint *Jane Smith*, my daughter, to be my executor." Make sure that there are not two names. In other words, the word "and" is not being used. It should always be, "In the event that a person is unwilling or unable to serve, *then I* appoint ..." This eliminates the need for two signatures on everything, and a total agreement by everyone in order to settle the estate.

However successor executors should always be named. If there is only one executor named and that person is unable or unwilling to serve, then the courts will have to appoint an executor to settle your estate. I oftentimes recommend that there be a successor executor named to the successor executor. Generally the first executor would be your spouse (if you are married). The second might be a child, and perhaps the third one might be another child or someone else.

Distributing Your Assets

I then ask people to consider the distribution of all of the assets that are being dispersed by the will. Everyone should have a clear idea of how their assets will be distributed. In other words, how much money is going to each person; what assets are they receiving? I always ask people that they use percentages rather than dollar amounts. In other words, Jane Smith is to receive 1 percent (1%) of my total assets; John Doe is to receive 2 percent (2%) of my assets. The dollar amounts will always be settled first, so if the estate has been depleted considerably, the dollar amounts will get paid first before it goes to the percentages. Using percentages will assure that the equality that you are trying to accomplish is maintained regardless of the value of your estate at the time of your death. Though the dollar value may fluctuate, the equality does not. Everyone gets the exact amount that you have determined appropriate. Don't worry about what your estate might be worth when the Lord calls you home; just use present value of your estate when you start to figure the percentages.

Delayed Inheritance

What do you do when you're not sure someone is responsible enough to receive a lump sum of money? I have found it very interesting (*and I have done a lot in this area*) that oftentimes a person may determine that they would like someone to receive money from their estate, but they feel that this person may not be responsible with the money. In a case such as this, I suggest that you leave that money to a charitable gift annuity for the income benefit of the individual. By doing so, you are assuring that for the lifetime of that individual they will have a monthly income. You can designate the age at which you would like that person to start receiving the income, and you are, therefore, avoiding the pitfall of them receiving a large lump sum of money and perhaps spending it foolishly.

Another area of consideration is that a spouse might want to leave their assets in a charitable trust for the income benefit of the grandchildren or the surviving spouse. This is another area of planning that is often overlooked in preparing a will. You get to do the Lord's work with more of your money, while providing a very valuable asset of income for life to a loved one. It's like leaving someone a retirement fund that will never run out of money as long as they live, and the income will never change.

Making Changes to Your Will

Did you know you can have a provision written into your will that states that this will can be changed by way of a letter written by you, and the executor must make an honest search, for stated period of time usually sixty days, for any such letter upon your death? Letters with the most recent date will be the letter recognized by the executor when it comes to distribution of these assets. This letter will have to be written and notarized and kept in a safe place. I would recommend, as I always do, that the executor of your will know where any such letter might be, along with knowing where the will itself would be. This can also save you a lot of money because it avoids the need to go back to the attorney to have an amendment made.

Knowing Your State's Tax Laws

It is important for you to understand that individual laws—tax laws and laws involved in settling estates—are very different. It is extremely
important that an attorney from the state in which
you live take time to draft and review your will.
I often prepare "rough draft" documents of wills
for people so they can have an idea of what they
need and, of course, to save them some money
when they eventually sit down with their attorney.
I always remind them that it is important for them
to note that this is a "rough draft" document, and
they need to take it to their attorney for the final
draft and approval. It is also important to understand that since laws are different state by state, if
you own property in a state in which you do not
reside, that property will have to be settled and
probated in that state. It does not fall under the
state of your residency.

Don't be misled to believe that just because all
of your property is in a joint name with someone
else, including your spouse, you will not need a
written will. Some people have said that the only

person who needs a will is the last person remaining under a joint–ownership situation. This is wrong; *everyone* needs and should have a will. Please keep in mind that your will can change as your life circumstances change, and a will continually needs to be updated. Also, remember that since individual laws in each state differ as to how assets are passed from spouse to spouse or even to your children, and as the law itself is changing continually—both tax law and estate planning law—oftentimes a will is read with an interpretation based on the current law. This could affect how your will gets settled.

Properly Executing and Notarizing Your Will

Even though your health may be failing and you are growing older, the courts will always honor the will of a person—as long as it is believed that they had a sound mind when creating the will, understanding exactly what he or she was doing. Also, although you may be physically and/or mentally sound and in complete understanding of what you are doing, a will can still be contested if it is believed that there has been some fraudulent representation or that someone has been under "undue influence" by someone close to them.

A will must always be executed properly and notarized, and all of the people signing the will must be in the presence of one another, which includes the witnesses. Witnesses do not have to be twenty-one years of age, but they must have the ability to understand that they are witnessing another person's signature. It is not necessary for a notary or a witness signing a will to know the content or the conditions of the will. I like to recommend, too, that if there is someone mentioned in the will that will receive a benefit from the will, they should not be a witness.

The Marital Deduction Benefit

There is a benefit called a "marital deduction." This allows a living or remaining spouse to preserve the tax benefit from the spouse who has died and adding it to the remaining spouse's estate tax credit. It is important that you note that this benefit can only be used if the will properly designates that it is to be used, and if there is a "marital deduction trust" (MDT) provision mentioned in the will so that a proper transfer of the assets can be made. I suspect that this provision will once again become a very useful tax–saving tool, since it would appear as though the current administration is likely to allow the tax law to expire in 2011, thereby lowering the tax credit on federal inheritance from three million to pre–Bush days, creating a real need for the MDT.

As I have already mentioned, it is important to understand that if a person has a living trust that the assets are to go to, the will becomes a very simple instrument classified as a "pour–over will" and does not have all the restrictions and details that a normal will should have. In these cases, it is important that you consult with your attorney so that the will does not restrict the ability of the trustees to work properly on behalf of the trust. Once again, make sure that if you have a living trust, you still have a will.

Finally, it is important that every three or four years, as your life circumstances change and the tax laws change, to regularly review your will. It is also important to note that you can reduce the cost of a will from an attorney by being well-prepared and having all the information well-documented and printed in a draft will that some organizations like mine will make available for you prior to going to the attorney. However, *please* do not try to avoid the cost of legal fees by doing it yourself. Seek professional counsel.

Giving to Children with Special Needs

Although this may not pertain to many people, there are some for whom this is very important. If you have an adult child or minor child that has special needs of some sort and is collecting state, local, or federal aid because of that disability, you must be very careful in planning your will and/ or trust. It is important that you have an attorney that is familiar with "special needs" trusts. A "special needs" trust can provide for the child—again, whether adult or minor—without affecting or risking them losing any state, local, or federal aid they may already be receiving. Do not just include them for a portion of your estate; make sure their distribution is left to the special needs trust.

Common Misconceptions about Wills

Before we close out the section on wills, I want to point out some very common misconceptions that many people have about wills. As I stated earlier, it is wrong for us to believe that only people with great sums of money—wealthy people or people who have a great deal of charitable bequests—need to have a will. We all need to have a will.

The other misconception is that it is only in times when you have children or other relatives that you feel are going to protest your last wishes, and you need to have a will to keep them from protesting. Having a will has never stopped anybody from contesting it or protesting against the provisions of the will. It becomes more important than ever, if that is your case, that a will is well thought out and drafted properly by an attorney. For example, I worked with a couple who have wanted to leave a child of theirs out of their will for a number of different reasons. In that case, I told them that they must put the child in the will for something, even if it is for one hundred dollars, so that this child cannot contest the will successfully. Chances are that a judge will say that obviously this person thought of you or they would not have left you the one hundred dollars. If you leave the person out of the will totally, they could argue to the court that you must have been under some undue influence or not thinking properly to have left out someone so important. (They will probably win.) This takes the argument away that "this person was obviously not in their right mind" because they did not even consider me in their will.

Conclusion

The cornerstone of all responsible estate planning is a will. If you have no other financial or estate planning tools or instruments, please make sure that you have a well–thought–out, well–defined, well–planned will. Remember, *everyone* needs a will. Even those with little to no assets or those with a living trust still need to have a will. Make sure that the distribution of your assets is clearly spelled out, that you identify an executor and guardian for minor children, make sure it is properly notarized, and that you are familiar with your state's current tax laws.

Also, do not neglect the importance of making a final tithe with your assets. This is an excellent opportunity to do the Lord's work one last time and continue to build a bigger kingdom.

Chapter Two

Power of Attorney

A Power of Attorney (POA) is a relatively easy estate–planning tool that allows you to transfer legal authority to someone else. Remember, a POA is a document that is used for your benefit while you are living and would allow a person you trust to take care of your day to day activities, usually due to a physical or mental incapacity, either temporary or permanent. You should always have a POA, along with a will. Oftentimes I tell people that a POA is more important than even the will itself. The POA will be the tool by which someone will be given the authority to handle your financial affairs and make any provisions that are necessary for you for a period of time that you may be disabled or in a situation where you are unable to do so yourself. The POA is only used while you are alive, however, and has no power at all after the Lord calls you home.

Naming Your Power of Attorney

Once you have determined who your executor is on your will, it is very likely that it will be the same trustworthy person that you would have as a power of attorney. Similar to your executors, the first power of attorney is generally your spouse, if you are married. As with executors, there ought to be named a successor power of attorney in the event that the initial person is unable or unwilling to serve as power of attorney. I always like at least two other people besides your spouse mentioned as potential power of attorneys.

What to Include in Your POA Document

The POA should be a carefully-constructed, well-written document. The POA should have the authority to make charitable contributions, manage your finances, pay your bills, make fiduciary responsibilities, and property management decisions, as well as dispose of property or asset decisions—all with the idea that they are to be made only to benefit you. It is also important that you mention items in your POA document such as trusted financial advisors. If your assets are being managed in a way that you are comfortable with, and you have faith and trust in the person that is managing those, I would suggest that the POA document does not allow for a power–of–attorney to change who those advisors are, unless it is absolutely necessary for effective care and management of your affairs. If you are naming a trusted financial advisor, you should always name the person by name and not that person's firm. This should be referred to as "the person" and the firm in which he or she is doing business. This eliminates any of your accounts falling into the hands of some other financial advisor, if the person that you are working with were to leave that firm. As you are beginning to start the process of estate planning, regardless of whether you plan on having a will, a trust, a revocable or irrevocable trust, a chartable trust, or a living trust, you must always have a POA.

The POA and the Living Will

Please note that this POA is very different from a living will. Most states now have adopted standard forms for living wills, and though I am not going to spend a lot of time talking about living wills here, I will say this: It is an absolute must for every single living person—and this has nothing to do with assets—to have a living will. Your wishes need to be known to those who are entrusted with your care in the event of a critical illness. Remember, the living will is only designed to honor your wishes in the case of terminal illness when it is agreed upon by more than one doctor that your death is very near and that it is impossible for that to change beyond an act of God. Only then is your living will appropriate. For prolonged disabilities, mental impairment, or coma situations, the POA should allow your power of attorney to make life-care decisions for you.

Conclusion

The POA is an essential instrument that enables you to transfer legal authority to another individual (usually your spouse) during a time in which you may be disabled or unable to make sounds decisions. Unlike a living will, which is only enforced once a terminal state has been declared, the power of attorney is used for extended periods of disability or mental impairment. It is an essential addition to any will and should be considered in your estate planning. A POA is an instrument that is used while you are living. There is a misconception that a power of attorney oftentimes has some sort of benefit to the estate once you pass away. Once the Lord calls you home, there is no need for a power of attorney. If you do not have a power of attorney and find yourself in need of one, the court through the state attorney generals office will appoint one, and there is no guarantee that it will be a person that you would want. As a matter of fact, you might not even know the person. That should be incentive enough to make sure you have a power of attorney in place.

Chapter Three

Living Trusts

Revocable and irrevocable

Be honest. How many of you reading this have a living trust and have no idea what it is for—all that you know is that it is bound up pretty in a very nice leather-bound binder. It's about two and a half inches thick, and you really don't know what's in there, but somebody convinced you (probably at a seminar) that you needed it; and, by the way, you probably paid too much for it. If that is you then the good news is, you are not alone. I meet people every single week in that exact same scenario. There are many lawyers doing seminars on living trusts that are not in the business of making sure you need one; and if you do, making sure that you understand why you should have one and how it works. Most of them are in the business of selling and printing documents.

The Benefits of a Living Trust

A living trust is a useful and sometimes a very advantageous estate–planning tool. I will tell you this—if you have one, and if you fall into that category of not knowing exactly what you have—having one will probably not ever hurt you or hurt your estate, but the question is, "Will it be advantageous for your estate? One of the real benefits of a living trust is that you can name trustees, and the trust is an addition to a will and can often help the executor or the trustees settle and distribute property a lot quicker and easier than they might do through a will.

Misconceptions about Living Trusts

One of the common mistakes that people make in creating a trust document is that they are boiler–

plate kinds of trusts that may have been bought at a seminar somewhere. Some of them are good; some of them are very bad—but the idea of just having a trust (good or bad) is not enough.

Making Your Trust Effective

In order for the trust to be effective, you must place your assets in the name of the trust. Assets such as your house, your investment accounts and bank accounts, savings and CDs, and others, need to be in the name of the trust. Remember, putting your assets in your trust does not cause you to lose control of the assets; it is true that you no longer own them, the trust does, but you have control of the trust as a trustee. Therefore, nothing changes; you still have complete oversight and management responsibilities and can continue to use the assets the way you did before they were placed in the trust. Also, part of the trust should list a time in which the trust assets will be distributed. There is a trigger mechanism that is used for disbursing the trust to the then living trustees. Often, the trigger mechanism is death. Now, remember, since the trust is distributing its assets to remaining trust-ees, there is no real *inheritance* taking place. This can oftentimes avoid Federal Inheritance Tax, if there would be Federal Inheritance Tax to begin with. I'll talk about that momentarily.

Once a trust is created by you and the assets transferred to the trust, then the trustee (also you) begins to manage those assets in the trust. Often they are managed the same way they were man-aged before they were placed into the trust. But the trust document might indicate how these assets are to be managed and by whom. During the lifetime of the trustees, the trust can distribute any income or even lump–sum assets to the trustees (you). But most often, upon death the trust is dissolved and distributed as outlined in the trust documents. That usually includes all the trustees and, of course, you have made a provision for a portion to be distruted to your favorite ministries, growing the kingdom. Keep in mind that you can change the provision of disbursements as often as you wish but once the trigging point has come (usually your death), no provisions can be changed.

If you are one who fits into that first paragraph and have an old trust in that leather binder that you got at the seminar you attended many years ago, that's okay. Just find it, blow the dust off, and go to your local attorney or any organization like mine and find out if you need it; if so, make the necessary changes so it will have a positive affect on your estate. If you haven't heard, it is now almost a definite that the current congress is going to allow the Bush tax credits to expire in 2011, which means that you may need that trust more than ever. A side note: I know this congress has a whooping 13 percent approval rating, but I haven't found anybody in that 13 percent—I guess they are out there somewhere. Okay, back to business.

A Special Needs Trust

I alluded back in the section on wills to a special needs trust. A special needs trust is a trust that is established to manage assets of an adult or minor child that has special needs or disabilities of some sort without affecting any financial help they may be getting from a government agency. This kind of trust is an extremely useful tool in assuring a provision that will not interfere with what they might already be getting. I have also set up a number of chartable trusts, making the income beneficiary the special needs person payable to a guardian to be used for their care. At the beneficiary's death, the remaining money in the trust will go to the ministry. For example: I recently faced a situation with an eighty–two–year–old woman that was the sole caregiver for her forty–year–old mentally handicapped son, Jason. She wanted all of her money to go to ministry but needed to make a provision for her son. I put all her money in a charitable trust and made her and Jason the income beneficiaries. When she goes to be with the Lord, the income for Jason will go to his power of attorney to be used for his care in a group home that he is currently in. When Jason dies, all her money is preserved for the kingdom. That is different then a special needs trust, but a great option.

Irrevocable Trusts

There are also trust documents that are established called irrevocable trusts. An irrevocable trust is set up and established with the idea of providing income and benefits to those trustees while they are living. The word irrevocable simply means that it cannot be changed or ended over the lifetime of the trust. It is important to note that in an extreme wealth management situation, irrevocable trusts can serve as a useful way to avoid taxes and also avoid the capturing of wealth by a nursing home. The IRS gives certain tax considerations to an irrevocable trust because it was established with the idea of being irrevocable and unchangeable. You have to think very carefully before establishing an irrevocable trust; there are going to be certain life-changing circumstances where you may need access to the assets and be unable to get access to them if they are in an irrevocable situation. I very seldom recommend that all of one's assets be placed into an irrevocable trust but there are definitely situations that warrant having this kind of trust. You have to consider whether the tax benefit outweighs the fact that it cannot be changed.

Conclusion

I believe that a well–thought–out and carefully–planned revocable living trust is a great planning instrument that can oftentimes help avoid different kinds of tax but, more importantly, can make the settlement of an estate extremely easy and quick for those trustees that have the responsibility of distributing assets and settling the estate. Remember, that having a trust is almost never a bad thing, but might not always be an advantage when it comes to saving taxes.

As always, remember the Lord's work as you think of the disbursements of your assets. Don't rely on one of the other trustees that are going to benefit from your trust to take care of the ministries that you feel passionate about supporting. Make sure you have outlined that support in your documents. After you're gone, the ministries that you love and have supported will continue to need financial support. Use what the Lord has blessed you with to see this work is done after you're home with him. God is counting on you and me to collaborate with him in growing the kingdom and seeing that the gospel gets proclaimed. No government tax program is going to offer that financial support; it is up to you and me.

Chapter Four

Charitable Trusts

Oftentimes we discount the use of charitable trusts in our estate planning. A charitable trust is one of the best ways, in my opinion, to increase your income dramatically from those appreciated stocks and appreciated assets that may be giving you a 2–3 percent dividend. Unfortunately, this year has seen highly appreciated assets become highly aggravating thorns in our side as they have turned upside down; but thorns too can bring relief when they are removed and used for income instead of indigestion. It is also an ideal way to do the Lord's work while you are living by giving to your own charitable trust and receiving an income from those assets while you are living. Keep in mind that upon your death, the remainder of these assets will be given to the ministries you have chosen.

What to Consider for Your Charitable Trust

One of the things that you should consider when you think of a charitable trust is that you can also use a charitable trust to make your final tithe prior to your death. Back in chapter one, I talked about the idea of committing 10 percent or more of your assets in a will to the ministries to which God leads you—a kind of final tithe. One of the ways, if you have the ability to do it now, is to make that final tithe today in a charitable trust so that while you are living, you can begin to receive the income benefit and receive a charitable deduction benefit. Here's how it might look:

Estimate how much will be going to the Lord's work upon your death. Say it is $50,000. And let's say your total portfolio of assets is now $500,000. It would probably make a lot of sense to peal out $50,000 dollars of assets, preferably assets that have little cost basis so that if you sold them it would create a big capital gains tax, and use those assets to create the charitable trust because since you are giving it to your chartable trust, you avoid any capital gain tax and begin to receive a minimum of 5 percent as income; but I manage trusts where people take a 6–7 percent return. If you used stocks to fund that chartable trust, the stock was probably returning 2 or 3 percent dividend return and that may be in jeopardy of going down or going away. Once the charitable trust is established, you can continue to make contributions to the trust throughout your lifetime or upon your death. Each time you make a contribution to your chartable trust, you get a tax deduction for a portion of your contribution and obviously your annual income will increase.

By making a charitable contribution at your death to your own charitable trust, you accomplish a number of things. One is that money you contribute to your charitable trust comes out of your estate pre–tax, thereby reducing the overall tax on your estate. Your charitable trust that you have now had established for a number of years will then dictate how that money is to be distributed. After the final contribution is made to your charitable trust, the fiduciary (the management organization or ministry that is managing your charitable trust) then makes those final distributions and closes the charitable trust. Also keep in mind that while you are living you can change the ministries that you wish to benefit as often as you like.

As I said in the opening of this chapter, it is incredible how many well–thought–out, well–defined estate plans totally miss the benefits of establishing charitable trusts. I think this is often due to the fact that so many lawyers, and even folks establishing the final estate plan, don't even consider the idea of giving away money—even though it may have a positive tax consequence to the final estate. More importantly, however, is the eternal value of doing kingdom work that is the real benefit to the believer.

I am not saying that a charitable trust should always be a consideration when planning your estate. What I am saying is that it is something that should be looked at carefully to determine whether it is appropriate for you at this time. In light of the current state of our economy and the financial markets, I am always encouraging people attending my seminars or listening to my radio program that if you are retired, secure permanent income that stays the same regardless of the market conditions. The *only* way you should consider doing that is through a charitable giving program—not ever through commercial means like insurance products. Remember, our goal is to the Lord's work.

The Charitable Gift Annuity

Since we are talking about charitable giving, I don't want to overlook the idea of a charitable gift annuity. Now, if you have listened to me for any length of time on the radio or have heard me speak, you know that commercial annuities are not something I would ever consider in an estate plan, or any other planning. But a *charitable* gift annuity, which guarantees you a lifetime income, is very different. First and foremost with a charitable gift annuity, upon your death, the remainder in the annuity goes to the ministry and not to an insurance company. Though you may love your insurance company (annuity company), don't let them have your money when you die; the Lord's work needs it—they don't. The other benefit is that you get a charitable deduction at the time you establish the charitable gift annuity.

There are several differences between a charitable gift annuity and a charitable trust. One is that the charitable gift annuity income stream never changes. It is a guaranteed, fixed amount every month for the rest of your life. The charitable trust is different in that the interest rate that you receive as income never changes for life; but each year the charitable trust is revalued, and the percentage which you have determined for income, say 5 percent a year, is going to be based on the new value. You need to keep in mind that the value of the trust, depending on how it is invested (and you should have choices on how it would be invested), can either be higher than it was in the previous year or it could be lower. Any charitable organization with whom you establish a charitable trust should give you a clearly–defined picture of how they invest their assets and what their previous track record has been in increasing or decreasing the value in their charitable trusts.

The Charitable Lead Trust

The other charitable instrument that is usually overlooked is the *charitable lead trust.* A charitable lead trust is an opportunity for you to make charitable gifts that provide immediate income for a ministry for a specific period of time. At the end of that period of time, the money that was used to establish this charitable lead trust (which, remember, has been providing income to the ministries of your choice) is returned to you or your beneficiaries, the idea here was to provide some income to the ministry for a time, not to give them a lump sum of money at a specific time.

For example, perhaps you designate a missions' agency—to which you have been contributing for a number of years—to support either specific missionaries or the missions' agency itself. You can designate a certain amount of funds into a charitable lead trust for ten years, after which every month the missions agency or the missionaries would receive the income that is established by the charitable lead trust. At the end of the ten–year period (and remember, per your instructions, this ten years could actually be fifteen or twenty, or until death), the remaining value of the trust is returned. This is a wonderful way to do the Lord's work for a specific period of time and still preserve principal for your heirs.

Conclusion

I would hope that as believers and as people who have continually supported the missions and the ministry of the kingdom of Jesus Christ, we would always consider continuing to give to missions or ministry in our estate planning. As you can see, there a number of ways and possibilities by which you can plan for your charitable giving as well as carefully planning for yourselves and your loved ones. Remember, it's about growing a bigger kingdom for Christ, not bigger barns for your heirs.

Chapter Five

Family Foundations or Donor Advised Funds

Years ago, many affluent families used a planning instrument called a "family foundation," and many of the wealthiest people in the country would establish one to which they, or other family members, could contribute their own money. They would then use this family foundation money to give to charitable causes. A family foundation can still be established, but there is a lot of regulatory burden and tax consequences and tax filings that go along with family foundations. They are, therefore, slowly becoming a thing of the past (or at the least a planning tool for only the wealthiest of families.)

Donor Advised Funds

In the place of family foundations, we now have a much easier and more logical planning tool: Donor Advised Funds (DAF). Donor advised funds can be established relatively quickly and easily through most charitable organizations, charitable foundations and even mutual fund companies. The donor advised fund works simply by establishing a fund in the name of your family; for example, the *Smith Family Donor Advised Fund*. This fund would give an opportunity for the family to gather and sit around the table, perhaps at Thanksgiving, and determine the recommendations they are going to make for the donor advised fund that year for their giving to ministry.

The thing I love most about donor advised funds is that it gives an opportunity for the others in a family to encourage the younger generations to continue the tradition of giving to the Lord's work. It is a wonderful opportunity for all the family members to contribute money through out the year, and even begin to get the younger children to participate in giving something every year to the family donor advised fund. Then, once a year, have a family meeting to determine what percentage of the donor advised fund will be given and to which ministries. I establish and manage many DAFs, and I recommend that if you establish a family DAF to do it with a recognized and established ministry. In most secular DAFs, you have to agree and understand that the fund will make some contributions to charitable organizations at their own discretion without counsel from you, so you need to be aware that they may be making contributions to organizations that are against our Christian values.

Conclusion

A donor advised fund can live on long after the initial establishment. It can be a perpetual fund that can be passed through generation after generation to keep the tradition and the biblical mandate of giving to the Lord's work.

The establishment of your family donor advised fund is relatively easy and can be estab-

Dan Celia

lished at most charitable foundations in ministry organizations.

DAF is a great alternative to the old family foundations; they are easy to establish, they are not just for the wealthy, and can be started with almost any amount of money by any person at any age. The regulatory burden of IRS filings are nonexistent for the you, so you and your family are free to continue to contribute as often as you would like and get a full tax deduction. Certainly, if you would like more information, you can check out my website for information on donor advised funds. This is also one of those opportunities to give to kingdom work to establish a wonderful teaching tool for generations to come that is often overlooked in our planning and our stewardship.

Chapter Six

Living Will or Advanced Health Directive

A living will gives you an opportunity to choose the extent to which you would like to receive life support or life through mechanical devices, as well as receiving medications and food and/ or water to sustain your life in a critical situation. Regardless of a power–of–attorney or a will, I believe that everyone should have a living will document that is on file with your doctor and possibly even one or two hospitals where it may be likely that you would go. Most states now have standard forms for what is called a "Living Will" or a "advanced health directive." It is important, as a part of your estate planning document and for all of your planning needs, that you have a living will, as I have stated earlier in chapter one. Certainly, your power–of–attorney should have a copy of your living will, as well as yourself.

Too often people forget that a living will only pertains to a terminal situation. In other words, two or more doctors would have to agree that there is no possible way, short of an act of God that in your current condition you could be healed or could live beyond a very short period of time. This "advanced health directive" or "living will" is only used in situations of the critically and chronically ill. It is never considered when there is a chance of recovery.

Conclusion

This living will document is oftentimes one that we have difficulty with or are not comfortable with reviewing and filling out. But I would urge all of you to understand how important it is for you to make these decisions. Don't put it on your children or anyone else. My wife is one of eleven children, and they all live within a twenty–five–mile radius of one another. When her father retired, he had his second open–heart surgery; before the surgery he did not talk to the admissions people at the hospital about making his wishes known just in case he did not come out of the surgery in good condition. He did well in the surgery and it appeared he would recover. One night while in intensive care his carotid artery ruptured, and it took health care professionals thirty minutes to get his heart functioning. Unfortunately he was on total life support with no brain function and no chance of recovery; for two weeks his children and my mother in–law agonized about what to do. His passing was surrounded by frustration and sometimes anger around the fact that they had to make a decision that he should have made. Please don't do that to your loved ones. It is more important than you think.

Chapter Seven

Long-term Care

This idea of long–term care and nursing homes seems to be more heavily on people's minds than ever before. Many of us, myself included, are at an age where we are caring for our aging parents.

From a biblical standpoint, it is such a privilege and honor that we should be able to care for our aging parents. But at the same time, we often think that we do not want our children to have to do the same for us, so we immediately think about nursing home care. From a personal point of view, my wife and I had my mother and father live with us for fourteen years. My mother went to be with the Lord eight years ago, and my father's health in the last four years has declined. Two months ago, at age ninety–six, my sisters and I had no other choice but to put him in a nursing home. There has not been a day that a family member does not spend a considerable amount of time with him in the home, but it was one of the hardest decisions I ever had to make, and I said to my wife, "I never want to do that to my children." I joke now with my two girls, both married, that when I am eighty, I am going to Africa to be a missionary, and I am going to do nothing but hold babies until the Lord calls me home; we should be so blessed.

Here are a couple of my insights in reference to long–term care insurance.

Overall, I believe in long–term care insurance. I think it is a great product, and I always believe that any time you can shift a risk for "pennies on the dollar" to an insurance company, it is a great thing. We all shift the risk of our house burning down by paying to have homeowner's insurance for just a few dollars compared to the value of our house. We insure the house just in case it should burn down, so we don't have to suffer the financial hardship of rebuilding our house. We obviously do the same thing with our car insurance and other types of insurance. It is always a good idea to shift the risk.

Our problem with long–term care insurance is that we do not know how likely the risk might be for us. The one thing for sure is that we all have a certain *immortality mindset*. We all believe that this is "certainly not going to happen to me. Either the Lord is going to take me before I require nursing home care, or I am just going to stay healthy right up until the day the Lord does take me home."

In my experience, what I have seen far too often is that somewhere around sixty–five or seventy years old, something happens, and we seem to have a *mortality check*. We might have a mild heart attack or a mild stroke, or fall and possibly break a bone, or have the need for a hip or knee replacement, and we suddenly realize that need for care or our death could very possibly happen to us. We could end up in that nursing home. However, if you start to think about long-term care insurance *after* such an event or after you have a health incident that puts you on prescription medications or creates an unhealthy situation in the eyes of an insurance company, long-term care insurance becomes *extremely* expensive.

When to Purchase Long-term Care

The time to be purchasing or looking for long-term care insurance is before the age of sixty-five and preferably when you are still healthy. Most long-term care insurance companies have finally realized over the last five years that all of the actuarial calculations and tables that they ran fifteen years ago have proven to be very inaccurate. The average stay in a nursing home is now a lot longer than thirty-three months, and modern medicine seems to be keeping us alive way too long, making the odds of paying out on the insurance policy a lot greater than the insurance companies originally anticipated. As a matter of fact, if as a married couple one of you lives to be eighty years old, statistically the odds are good that you will need some sort of skilled nursing or long–term care. So the probability of you needing long–term care is a lot greater then your house burning down. Since we are quick to insure our house, why not insure our care?

When Not to Purchase Long-term Care Insurance

There are certainly situations in which we do not need long–term care insurance. If we have very few assets and very little savings, then long–term care insurance is probably not an issue. If we are already living on a very fixed income and struggling, you certainly don't need to add a long–term care insurance payment to that mix. The fact of the matter is, we will probably run through our assets quickly and are likely to end up on the roles of Medicaid. On the other hand, if we have enough wealth and enough income, oftentimes that income and investment strategy can be enough to take care of our needs. In that case, I would not waste the money for long–term care insurance.

The other situation, of course, is for those who are not wealthy. Either their income can not provide for their long–term care, or they who have little or no assets in which Medicaid is the logical option; there are also those who are somewhere in between the two. Generally these are the people for whom long–term care insurance is appropriate. I always suggest, because it is so expensive, that one of the things you may consider doing is to play the statistics—play the odds. The odds are that the woman is the one who is going to need long–term care, if you are a married couple. Statistically what happens is that the man dies first, so he, therefore, tends to need care first, and the wife is likely to be the caregiver, thereby keeping him out of a nursing home situation. The problem is, that after the Lord calls the husband home, the wife oftentimes has no one to care for her, and she ends up in a situation where she might need the long–term care. One of the things you can do to reduce your expenses is play the odds and just get one long–term care policy on the wife.

Our assets need to be gone to qualify for Medicaid

The other thing that we hear a lot about, particularly from our neighbors and friends and some other advisors, is that we should spend our money down. If we are in this middle area, we are often told to spend our money or to give it away, thereby qualifying us for Medicaid sooner than we might if we allow the money to go to our care or the nursing home as opposed to our heirs. I am not completely against this idea. I think all of us at a certain age ought to have a program by which we are gifting our money to our heirs and to the Lord if it is appropriate, thereby getting those dollars out of our estate. I always think that it's a better idea for your heirs and the kingdom to receive that money while you are living, as opposed to taking the chance that nursing care could spend it. But keep in mind that there is a five–year look–back period from Medicaid and from the IRS, so Medicaid could look at your gifting in the last five years and claim that you were gifting that in order to avoid paying for the cost of the nursing care, and they can then recapture those dollars. Also, it may be difficult to get into a nursing home straight from home to Medicaid so have some resources to be able to get in as a private pay patient. Once you're in, it is unlikely that you will be put out. So, if a gifting program is in order for you, and you would like to gift your money to ministries and heirs, you have to be thinking about this five–year look–back period. In general, I always like the idea of getting as much money out of your estate as possible.

Also, all of those things that I have already mentioned in the trust section on giving would apply to assets that you have. It may be advantageous for you to use your assets, if you have no heirs, in creating a charitable trust. In doing that, it is likely that Medicaid will not recapture the lump sum asset, but they will be able to use the income that the trust generates to pay your expenses. Upon your death, however, by doing this you will guarantee that the ministries you care about will still receive the remainderment of that trust and the Lord's work will still get done.

How to Shop for Long-Term Care

I often find that people buy long–term care insurance based on price and not on whether the company is reputable. There are a few companies that I would recommend, but for the most part, you have to know how to shop for long–term care.

1. Always get a daily benefit that is close to the going rate in your area for daily care. Unfortunately, requiring or asking for a rate that is close to the existing rate of daily care in our area can be an expensive option.

2. You should always get an inflation rider on that daily rate so the daily rate continues to increase as the policy ages, thereby keeping pace with inflation. This is also a very expensive option but in my opinion a must.

3. Make sure that the long-term care policy always pays the same rate for in-home care, if it becomes necessary. That too is an option that can increase the expense of the policy.

4. Always make sure that no more than three ADLs (Activities of Daily Living)—there are usually five of them—are triggered in order to make a payout. The five of these are generally: "cognitive" or lucidness function, such as Alzheimer's. This is generally one that most plans provide for the benefit to be triggered if this one of the five is present. The other four are toileting, dressing, transferring from chair to bed, and eating without help, in which three, including cognitive, must be triggered in order to make a payout. The cognitive ADL is usually the only ADL that will trigger payout by itself. Generally a payout won't begin until at least three of the five are present. Don't get a policy that requires four, or one that does not include cognitive as a single qualifier.

5 . And finally, make sure that the policy is going to continue to pay for a minimum of three years of nursing care before it stops. The ideal policy is one that has a lifetime payout, but again, with each one of these options, the premium becomes more and more expensive. Keep in mind all of that expense could be paid, and you may never need the care.

Concerns Regarding Long-Term Care

One of the concerns that I have for long–term care policies is that far too often people get a policy and think they are covered but don't actually have enough coverage to make any difference when it comes to preserving the money in their estate. A common misconception is that we must have long–term care insurance to pay all of our nursing care expenses. This is mainly because of the fear that if one of us, as a married couple, would go into a nursing home, Medicaid or the nursing home would take our home away. Keep in mind that as long as one of you remains in the house, they cannot take that home from you, nor can they deplete your income so low that you cannot live in the "community," as they call it.

You see, if you price out LTC insurance, and you express to the salesperson that it is too expensive, the salesperson can customize a long–term care policy to almost make it as affordable as you would like. But be careful; in doing that you will be eliminating some of the options that I have just pointed out, and you could end up with a policy that will be of little help. As you begin to lower your daily benefit, take away the inflation rate, reduce the time that the policy will pay out, increase the ADLs that it takes to trigger a payout, chances are the policy may come within a reasonable cost that you can afford. Unfortunately, you may be paying for a policy that is of little help should you need long–term care. I hope one of your goals is to preserve some of what God has blessed you with for his work. If it is purchased correctly, long–term insurance can do that.

A Long-Term Care Plan

About ten years ago I developed a plan called the Regency Care Plan. It was something that I developed as a very simple plan to pay for long–term care and do the Lord's work at the same time. I believe it is the only way to buy long–term care insurance and should be a part of your planning if you are able to do it. The idea of the care plan is to shop for long–term care insurance and determine the policy and the payment for the insurance. Once the payment is established, take a look at purchasing a charitable gift annuity—not a *standard* commercial annuity, but a *charitable gift* annuity. You can possibly fund a charitable gift annuity to the amount that will pay the premium on the long–term care insurance. Here are a number of benefits to doing it this way:

1. It is a *one–time* payment to the charitable gift annuity.

2. The money you put into the charitable gift annuity will, upon your death, go to the Lord's work.

3 . You immediately receive a tax deduction for establishing the charitable gift annuity, and some organizations, such as The Regency Foundation, will gladly pay the annual premium with the proceeds from the annuity to the long–term care insurance company.

You do the Lord's work, you get a tax deduction, and if for some reason you no longer want the insurance or the Lord has called one of you home and your premium is reduced, you get the balance as income.

I believe that one of the best benefits of the Regency Care Plan is the policy will continue to pay your long–term care insurance long after you reach an age where you feel as though you would no longer like to pay the premiums. Sometimes I call that the age where you get a little cranky and feel like this is far too much money for something you're never going to need or don't care if you need it. You need to understand that insurance companies count on you doing just that, dropping the policy after paying premiums for years. They might even send you a thank you note. The charitable gift annuity eliminates that possibility and, generally, the person totally forgets they even have the long–term care insurance once they establish the charitable gift annuity.

Conclusion

Once again, if you are considering long–term care insurance, I hope you will consider doing it while continuing to build the kingdom by way of funding a charitable gift annuity. Also, the vast majority of the states in this country issue a brochure on purchasing long–term care insurance. Contact your State Insurance Commission to receive a copy of that pamphlet.

I am a believer in shifting the risk of nursing home care and skilled nursing to a long–term care insurance provider, but you really need to do your homework, get a good policy, and think about all the statistics while understanding your own financial situation to determine whether or not you will need this kind of policy.

Chapter Eight

Planning for Tax Reasons

Obviously, developing a well–thought–out plan for our estate and for how we will live during our retirement years is a very critical part of the planning process. It is certainly something that I believe *biblically* we are called to do Proverbs 15:22 is the foundation verse to my ministry: *Without counsel, plans go awry, But in the multitude of counselors they are established.* In other words, we are called to plan and to seek counsel if we are to be successful in our stewardship. We are also called to take care of those that are under our roof, which might be ourselves in our retirement years, and we are certainly called to continually give to kingdom work. I believe that we ought to take advantage of all the laws and pay only the taxes that we absolutely have to pay. We certainly want to plan so that there will be an ease for those executors and trustees settling our estate, and most importantly, to make sure that when the Lord calls us home, things are carried out exactly as you or I would want them to be carried out.

I am sure I don't have to tell you that we are going to see major revision over the next three or four years in Estate Tax Law. Many of those revisions may be based on a need to raise taxes or do away with tax brakes in order to pay the debt we have created. In 2001 Congress enacted new legislation that made substantial changes to the Gift and Estate Tax Law. Many of these provisions in the 2001 Tax Act were to be phased in over nine years. That was to begin in 2002. My wish would be that the 2001 Tax Act that is almost completely phased in would be made permanent. We know now that is not going to happen. The estate tax "phasing in," or what you might call "phasing out," schedule looks like this:

Estate Tax Schedule

Year	Tax Exempt Amount	Maximum Tax Rate
2002	$1,000,000	50%
2003	$1,000,000	49%
2004	$1,500,000	48%
2005	$1,500,000	47%
2006	$2,000,000	46%
2007	$2,000,000	45%
2008	$2,000,000	45%
2009	$3,500,000	45%
2010	Tax Repealed	0%

It is important to note that in 2011, the Tax Rate Schedule reverts back to pre-2002. It is likely, therefore, that the repeal in 2010 is only going to last for one year.

I have been saying for years that congress has to do very little to raise taxes substantially or to increase income from taxes substantially. They simply have to do nothing; in case you have not noticed, Congress is often very good at doing nothing, so the idea of increasing taxes dramatically by a new administration is not going to be a matter of just trying to get new legislation passed. They need only to do nothing, and if they do nothing, the tax law will revert back to the old, thereby *increasing* taxes for a large segment of our tax paying people.

I have chosen not to go into great detail on all of the tax laws, knowing certainly that they would change and that some of them are far too complex to detail in this book. But I will say that it is more important than ever that you have aligned yourself with a planning professional and an attorney. One of the best places to start is with the ministry that you would like to continue to work with.

Oftentimes these ministries, such as our ministry, have people within their organization—lawyers or planners—that can help you through your estate planning from a biblical perspective.

One thing that is certain is that you have no chance of taking advantage of all that the law provides unless you seek counsel. Though there are many rules and regulations in the IRS Codes that allow individuals to avoid certain taxes, they are not widely publicized or simple to institute. As people that are concerned about our stewardship and planning, it would be foolish not to consider the entire scope of the tax law so that we can do our best to avoid taxes that legally we have the right to avoid. When passing our estate from generation to generation, there are specific generation–skipping taxes that, though complex, can easily be incorporated in one's estate plan so that some of these taxes can be avoided.

We are not to plan only to avoid taxes. As a matter of fact, it is amazing how some of the wealthiest individuals I know, and some of the greatest givers I know, have little concern with avoiding taxes. Their hearts are truly to do the Lord's work.

As we all strive to hear those words, "Well done, good and faithful servant," we need to make sure that our estate planning is done well.

I am always available for consult, free of charge, to anyone interested in trying to wade through the complexities of estate planning. I know that many of my colleagues in other ministries are also prepared to do that, and I certainly—as I have already said—would suggest that you contact someone to start your planning on the foundation of a biblically-sound organization that has your best interest at heart.

I know that much of the tax law seems very complicated, but again, this is all the more reason for us to plan wisely as we go through some of the tools that are allowed by law for us to have in place. Utilize all of the planning instruments that are appropriate for you to not only save taxes, but to ensure that when the Lord calls you home, and even while you are living, things are being carried out the way that you choose.

I hope that all of these things will continue to encourage you and help you, to plan wisely as you stay focused on growing the kingdom and not just building bigger barns.

Conclusion

There are so many more technical kinds of programs and products and ways of planning that need to be considered. This is all the more reason for you to partner with an attorney or an estate-planning professional that can help you think through all these possibilities. I hope that the professional help which you seek out would be that of a godly individual. Remember Proverbs 15:22 (NIV), *"Plans fail for lack of counsel, but with many advisers they succeed."* It is important that you understand that regardless of your financial situation, there needs to be some level of planning—whether it is simply having a will, a power-of-attorney and a living will, or whether it is having numerous living trusts, charitable trusts, and other kinds of planning vehicles because of a very complex and large estate.

We all need to be seeking godly counsel and taking all of these plans before the Lord in prayer to find a balance between building larger barns and giving to kingdom work. Be prudent and wise in your planning so that not only *your* goals are accomplished, but more importantly, *God's* will for the resources with which he has provided us is accomplished.

God's plan for each and every one of us is certainly different, but there are certain things that God does will and purpose in our lives. One of them is to be certain that with all the resources with which the Lord has blessed us, whether they are a lot or a little, we make every effort possible to see that the gospel is proclaimed. God wants his people to continue to give to his work here on earth. One thing is for certain: we are not, in all of our planning, to eliminate any of our giving to the kingdom. We are not to eliminate or stop working—whether it be by giving of our time or money—to kingdom work. We are not to set aside the visions that God has given us to partner with him to do his work. We need to always remember that we are instruments of God's love and peace here on earth. We are his tools to cultivate, to seed, to plant, and to bring in a harvest for the kingdom of God. All of our estate plans should include doing God's work with the wealth, talents, and the abilities he has given us. While developing a sound, prudent, well-thought-out plan for our financial future is a good idea, if this includes the elimination of God's work, then the plan is not of God. Be sure to ask God for discernment as you pray about your future and your present planning. Take all of this to him in prayer with an open heart, an open mind, open ears, and most importantly, an open hand. Let go; it's not yours.